WHEN WE DRIFT

WHEN WE DRIFT
COPYRIGHT © 2021 JUSTIN WILLIAMS

All rights reserved. No part of this book may be used or reproduced by any means, graphic, electronic, mechanical, including photocopying, recording, taping, or by any information storage retrieval system without the written permission of the author except in the case of brief quotations embodied in critical articles and reviews.

Unless otherwise indicated, all Scripture quotations are taken from the King James Version @1979 by Thomas Nelson. Scripture taken from the New King James Version. Copyright © 1982 by Thomas Nelson, Inc. Used by permission. All rights reserved. Scripture quotations marked (NASV) are taken from The New American Standard Version, NASB © 1960, 1962, 1963, 1968, 1971, 1972, 1973, 1975, 1977 Lockman Foundation. Scripture quotations marked Scripture quotations marked (AMP) are taken from The Amplified Bible, AMP © 2015 Lockman Foundation.
Quotations marked (TPL) are taken from The Passion Translation®. © 2017 Broad Street Publishing® Group. Scripture quotations are from the ESV® Bible (The Holy Bible, English Standard Version®), © 2001 by Crossway, a publishing ministry of Good News Publishers. Used by permission. All rights reserved.

Typesetting by tall pine

ISBN: 978-1-7353469-9-1

*Published in the United States of America

WHEN WE DRIFT

THE GUIDE TO TAKING BACK
THE LIFE YOU ALWAYS WANTED

JUSTIN WILLIAMS

This book is a final farewell to an initial lie that splintered into multiple lies, which introduced an imposter and led me to drift far off the path I wanted to walk. I dedicate these pages, my story, and this guide to all of you who are ready to say farewell to the drift that has caused you to lose your way. The path back to your true identity and life purpose exists. We are going to find it together in the pages before you.

PART 1: THE BACKSTORY

MY STORY — 2

PART 2: WHAT IS THE DRIFT?

AMANDA'S STORY — 10
THE IMPOSTER THAT EMERGES — 14
DAVID'S STORY — 18
ME: TRUTH, WORTH, AND BLAME. — 21
WHAT FEELS TRUE BECOMES TRUE, EVEN IF IT'S NOT — 27
IT'S NOT YOUR FAULT — 30
HOW CAN YOU OVERCOME THE DRIFT — 36
WHAT TO EXPECT — 39

PART 3: THE CLUES

CLUE NUMBER ONE: WHAT DO YOU NEED? — 42
ASKING THE WRONG QUESTIONS — 45

PART 4: THE EXERCISES

EXERCISE 1 - 10 WORST MOMENTS — 54
EXERCISE 2 - THE LIES — 57
EXERCISE 3 - VOWS — 63
EXERCISE 4 - THE IMPACT — 69
EXERCISE 5 - THE NEVER ENDING CYCLE — 75
EXERCISE 6 - WHAT'S THE TRUTH? — 82

RECESS

PART 5: WHAT NEEDS TO CHANGE?

THE CONTRACT — 100
FOR FURTHER REFLECTION — 106
NOW WHAT? — 112
A WORD ABOUT ME — 114
NOTES — 119

PART ONE:
THE BACKSTORY

"I used to be Snow White—but I drifted."

—Mae West

MY STORY

Adrenaline was pumping through my body like a racehorse ready to shoot out of the gate. Ready to fight, I headed straight to the parking lot of my Dallas apartment complex.

The sun had gone down, but it was August in Texas and I immediately broke into a sweat. The summer heat was just below the boiling point, causing tree sap to drip and cover my car like caramel on a candy apple. I was overheating inside and out. Panic attacks had stolen eight years of my life and counting. My life felt like one long boxing match, one in which I was fighting myself round after round and constantly losing.

Years of counseling had not worked. Neither did alcohol, pornography or the prescription pills that could numb my senses within minutes, which I carried everywhere, folded up in a small piece of paper safely tucked away in my jeans' pocket. My vices helped me to cope and assured me that this was all normal.

I stared down at faded lines of parking spaces on the worn pavement, deciding whether to pace, yell or both. I was angry. I'd been angry for a long time. I wasn't the person I wanted to be. I wasn't where I thought I should be in life at the age of thirty. The person I had always wanted to be was nothing more than a distant memory, a childhood dream. I had become a highly functional addict and imposter, who hid insecurities, anxiety and panic behind defense mechanisms of denial and humor. In sober moments, with lucid thoughts and authentic desperation, I allowed myself to feel the disappointment of my reality and became angry enough to muster an ounce or two of energy to offensively fight for the life I wanted.

"This ends tonight," I would say, both to myself and to the panic attack rising within.

I was determined that I could go head to head with it and win this time. My fingers curled into fists; I was ready. I paced back and forth in the empty parking lot, pumping my fists to the sky and swinging my arms like I was holding an invisible sword. I rattled off all the affirming statements, positive declarations and spiritual proverbs I had been told in therapy over the past eight years, advice that promised to work if I only believed them. I tossed them aimlessly into the darkness, hoping to hit some undiscovered target of breakthrough.

The swearing and swinging wore me down to a puddle of contradictions. The confidence I had started with evaporated into despair, and I began pleading to God in prayer to have mercy and do something. Intervene. Rescue me. Rapture me. Or let me die. Years of panic attacks on the regular would break anyone, and I was no different. If anything, I was past the point of being broken. My knees hit the pavement. I wanted to lie down, sink beneath the asphalt and pass into another life.

I could almost hear dark angels, my personal mental and spiritual enemies, laughing at me as they buzzed around in the air, taunting my loss. They had a sizable yet easy victory over me that day. They always did. My fight did not last long before I felt completely defeated. I couldn't hide from the significant reality at hand: I didn't believe half of what I claimed to believe, and the words I hurled into the air held no real power.

Outwardly, I was a thirty-year-old, grown man. Inwardly, I was a scared kid, emotionally locked in my teen years, a time when my parents divorced and kids at school started using me as a verbal punching bag. As much as I wanted a breakthrough, deep down, I believed I deserved a life of panic attacks.

I had consulted with a handful of professionals over the years—counselors, psychiatrists, and anxiety specialists. I had my childhood memorized, thoroughly dissected inside and out. I spent a lot of good money and emotional effort, but was still at ground zero, no further along than when it all began, eight long years earlier.

A SUBTLE DRIFT

The moment you buy into a lie about your identity or value, no matter how big or small, you begin to drift. You slowly drift off your path and become someone you never thought you would be, lost to the degree that you no longer know how to get back. The person you had always wanted to be is now a far-off fairytale, faded in the distance, and you reason the person you aspired to be was nothing but a childish dream. That was foolish; this must be real life.

It's subtle for most people—a slight bump that knocks you one degree off center. But left unattended, forgotten, unchecked and undealt with, it compounds over time and can leave you 30, 60, or even 90 degrees off course. How many degrees off course are you? How far have you drifted?

I was just fourteen years old when my drift began. My parents' marriage was falling apart, and I believed the lie that I wasn't worth enough to them to stay together. I also assumed I was partly to blame for their marital tensions. I had spent most of my childhood with a bar of soap in my mouth for saying something too colorful, and I got walloped by my dad's belt if I did something worse. Being rebellious was the strategic way I had discovered to attract the attention of others, even if it was negative attention.

In adolescence, I surmised that my ability to shoot myself in the foot with my bad behavior was the reason my parents were tiptoeing around conversations about whether or not to stay together. I rationalized that I was part of the problem that caused stress to seep into their relationship, stressors that ultimately caused the seams of their marriage to unravel. I also rationalized that if I had the ability to screw up everything then I could also fix it. All I needed to do was become invisible. If I was the problem, then I simply had to remove myself from the equation and disappear. So that's what I did, or attempted to do.

Unfortunately, in my futile attempt to become invisible, I unknowingly divorced myself from my innate value. Not knowing, believing or living from my value left my identity vulnerable to further lies that splintered my self-worth. A single lie would stay tucked away in the back of my mind, dragging me further off course. Soon, another lie would enter, such as, I'm a loser or No girl will ever want to marry me. This cycle of lies compounding lies lodged in my thoughts and manifested in my feelings and unhealthy behaviors, allowing me to drift further away into becoming someone whom, eventually, I could no longer recognize.

It weighed on me like a semitruck carrying a load of elephants. What started as a subtle drift escalated into a gap the size of the Grand Canyon between who I wanted to be and who I had become. It took years for me to even notice. I found myself having moments of contradiction in which I was able to present myself as one who had it all together, while under the hood, I was a sailboat adrift without a sail, so far off course from the path I wanted to travel. I was miserable and hiding under a canopy of coping mechanisms.

At one point in my early twenties, I lived in a small garage apartment and slept on an ugly futon my parents bought me. Yes, it was literally a garage with a cheap A/C unit duct-taped to a flimsy window that sputtered along as the Texas heat mocked me. I didn't want to be here. I didn't know how my life had gotten to this point. I had a low-paying job, a lack of deep friendships, and an extra twenty pounds I couldn't hide from my mom, who always brought it up whenever I saw her. I was far from the person I wanted to be or the place I thought I should be in life.

Sound familiar?

PART TWO:
WHAT IS THE DRIFT?

"A lie gets halfway around the world before the truth has a chance to get its pants on."

—Winston Churchill

AMANDA'S STORY

What is it for you? Painful experiences, disappointments, lies believed along the way, rejection, a break-up, divorce, abuse, wounds from your parents, tragedy, life circumstances, getting fired, trauma, loss of a loved one? These are the forks in the road, which, if left unacknowledged and unprocessed, will lead to drift. These are the micro-moments that turn into macro-drift. The result?

We cope.

We settle.

We check out.

We numb.

Globally, alcohol consumption is up 70 percent since 1999.[1] Pornography websites get more visitors each month than Netflix, Amazon and Twitter combined.[2] Wives are cheating on their spouses 40 percent more frequently than they did in 1990.[3] Diagnoses of anxiety disorders are through the roof, affecting nearly 300 million people,[4] and depression is now the leading cause of disability in the world.[5] Marijuana is becoming more socially acceptable, and every year, more states are jumping on the bandwagon by legalizing it.

This isn't normal. This isn't the design for you, or for anyone. These statistics tell a tragic story of drift, away from wholeness, connection, self-worth and meaningful contribution.

Amanda's drift wasn't as obvious. She appeared to have it all together. She graduated at the top of her class after a full-ride scholarship to Cornell University. She was not only bright, but she was also stunning. She shot down most guys with their failed pick-up lines. She studied law and, upon passing the bar examination, was quickly recruited to work for a prestigious New York City law firm.

I was shocked when she opened up to me one day over coffee. We'd been friends for years and always had good conversations, but never about her drift. Based on all her achievements, I never would have suspected she drifted at all.

"I'm finally doing exactly what my parents have always wanted," she told me.

Her words were sharp and the look on her face reflected her parents' disappointment in her. She rolled up her sleeve to reveal the years of punishment she had inflicted on herself with a razor blade, attempting to alleviate the tension between being herself and living the life her parents wanted. My heart raced just looking at the scars she had inflicted to remind herself that she wasn't good enough. I could not understand. But Amanda did.

Her father had always wanted a boy, but he got a girl. Unknowingly, the bar of worthiness he set in that family was high—too high for anyone to actually attain. Her 1490 SAT score fell short. Any score would have fallen short, because, ultimately, she knew deep down that she wasn't what her father wanted. The pressure to be perfect bled out in every area of her life. Amanda needed to look perfect, feel perfect and perform perfectly.

After all, if she was not what her father had wanted, logic told her, *You're not what anyone wants. You don't hit the mark. You're not good enough.* And these lonely, painful thoughts grew into the suffocating belief that in order to survive in life, she had to hit all the marks and be the picture of perfection. Obsessive control and performance became the name of Amanda's game.

The pain of being a disappointment to her father created a hole as big as the galaxy in every compartment of her heart. Because she didn't know how to stop the pain, she spent most of her teenage years trying everything from self-sabotage to self-harm. Amanda wasn't even battling against herself anymore. She had succumbed to an imposter, a "perfect" version of the Amanda she believed people wanted her to be. She couldn't believe anyone would accept the *real*

Amanda, so she surrendered to this imposter and drifted into an impossible hole to climb out of. Terrorized by thoughts of rejection and abandonment if she didn't keep up her perfect pace, she remained in hiding, isolated from the intimacy of anyone knowing or accepting her real feelings, thoughts and desires.

I could replace Amanda with any number of names. Could I replace it with your name? Do you face a constant panic cycle of failing, of not being seen or truly known, or of being rejected and abandoned? A fear of what others may think or say about you will pull you away from healthy relationships, career aspirations and self-acceptance. That's the drift.

We all drift. I can hear it in the language people use.

"I'm not **who** I thought I **would** be, or **where** I think I **should** be."

It always involves the same combination of those words: **who**, **would**, **where** and **should**. Why is it that we rarely ever hear people say they are living the life they always wanted to live?

THE IMPOSTER WHO EMERGES

When you drift, an imposter emerges to help you cope. It takes over your life, divorcing you from your identity, sending you off course and into denial structures that numb the pain caused by the wound that started your drift. Author Brennan Manning elaborates on the imposter in the second chapter of his book *Abba's Child*:

> The false self buys into outside experiences to furnish a personal source of meaning. The pursuit of money, power, glamour, sexual prowess, recognition, and status enhances one's self-importance and creates the illusion of success. The imposter is what he *does*.
>
> Imposters are preoccupied with acceptance and approval. Because of their suffocating need to please others, they cannot say no with the same confidence with which they say yes. And so they overextend

themselves in people, projects, and causes, motivated not by personal commitment but by the fear of not living up to others' expectations.

The imposter prompts us to attach importance to what has no importance, clothing with a false glitter what is least substantial and turning us away from what is real. The false self causes us to live in a world of delusion.

The imposter is a liar.

There it is in black and white. "The imposter is a **liar**." Acknowledging the truth of that statement can be the beginning of your freedom. The imposter convinces us to:

- Live in fear.
- Focus wholly on the acceptance and approval of others.
- Feel blind to the light and truth of our own emptiness and hollowness.
- Demand to be noticed and crave compliments.
- Gain identity and status from achievements and connections with "important" others.
- Lack true intimacy in all relationships—with ourselves, others and God.
- Try to come across as important. (That one stings, right?)
- Dread solitude and silence with no distraction.
- Be hard on ourselves and project fear and anger onto others.
- Lack gentleness and compassion toward ourselves and, as a result, toward others.

My imposter emerged as a class clown, the funny guy who used humor to gain others' acceptance and cover the pain I was feeling. He helped me distance myself from the questions that asked if I would ever amount to anything or become anyone significant. The imposter creates defense mechanisms (for me, humor; for Amanda, perfect performance) to avoid thoughts that bring self-awareness and the potential of change. The imposter loves self-sabotage—setting yourself up to fail in order to reinforce how you already feel about yourself.

Amanda gave the impression that no guy was good enough for her. The walls around her true self were so high that she never had a single significant relationship and, instead, settled for a lonely life, when all she wanted was to be loved and accepted by someone else. In her drifted reality, self-sabotage was easier to endure than to face the lies that fueled her fears and stacked a ton of bricks around her heart, her soul, and, ultimately, her true and liberated identity.

Brennan Manning concludes, "Grace and compassion for self get discarded as being soft. Besides, you don't deserve it. The imposter whispers, you don't deserve that good life, or good friends, the job you want and vacations by the sea."

So, we play a game and hide behind the curtain. After all, it feels safer being a spectator of life rather than an active participant.

Simply put, the imposter presents itself as a solution to our pain, when in truth, it suppresses the pain.

The drift wants you to become stuck, and to stay stuck. It sets you on a shelf of insignificance to collect dust. Often, those around you are also drifting. They may not take notice that you are stuck because they are also stuck. You are terrified to tell others that you might be stuck in the drift. It feels scary to admit you need help. You wonder, *How will they respond?* It reminds me of when I met David.

DAVID'S STORY

David took odd jobs for years after graduating college and had finally settled in working at a coffee shop. When I met him, he had over twelve years as a barista under his belt. He lived a simple life of microwave dinners and video games at night. I couldn't imagine this was the life of his dreams. He didn't seem fulfilled and thriving. I started asking questions to see what might be under the surface. The questions peeled back his story to find a theme emerging.

His dad always came across as uninterested in David, even though they seemingly had a cordial relationship. They lived only twenty-five minutes from one another, but his dad seemed content to only see David when he showed up every couple months.

David's father had never put pressure on him to be anything

great growing up. He didn't encourage David to be anything, really. As a kid, David tried every sport possible, multiple musical instruments and even theater, unknowingly trying to light a spark of interest from his dad. He would join his dad at his workbench in the garage, offering to help, trying to learn, wanting to enjoy a hobby together. As much as he didn't enjoy watching auto racing, David spent hours with his dad in front of the TV, asking him questions about the drivers and their stats, hoping to be accepted into his dad's world, looking for any connection that would affirm he was valuable. In high school, David would occasionally comment about applying for a job or possibly asking out a girl, hoping his dad would ask questions or encourage him. His dad was never mean or cruel but neither did he appear interested or excited about anything David did.

Eventually, David lost any confidence that he was worth being around. His dad didn't appear to believe in him, so David didn't believe in himself either. He had been given no reason to do so. The imposter who emerged and took over David's life had little worth to others, and told David he had nothing to offer of significance. As a kid, he had always dreamed of being a musician, but his Starbucks paycheck felt a more accurate measurement of his worth, and so he had long abandoned the idea of making a career in music.

To this day, David continues to work as a barista while daydreaming of life on a music tour or of being a studio musician or songwriter. It's the drift. It sits you on the sidelines and convinces you to remain a spectator. The drift is the subtle difference between someone who becomes a rock star and someone who stays a barista, all the while dreaming of what could have been and believing that it's too late to pursue. It could have been different for David, but his drift compounded over time and the thought of changing his life trajectory seems irrational at best.

Some of you may argue, "There's nothing wrong with being a barista!" That may be true for you, but it's not true for David. He didn't grow up dreaming of slinging espresso shots and scraping by, paycheck to paycheck. It would be a different narrative if his job as a barista was a stepping stone to something he wanted. David, however, doesn't want to risk stepping toward anything else beyond espresso shots. He is too afraid to step toward the men's group at his church, or his cute coworker, or the open mic night at his favorite bar, all because he believes he isn't good enough, smart enough, funny enough or attractive enough to be of interest to anyone. His drift has landed him alone and numb.

ME: TRUTH, WORTH AND BLAME

After I graduated college, massive panic attacks the size of forty-foot tidal waves sounded an internal alarm that there was a problem. They served as a reminder that my life was out of control and dictated the direction I would go. I wasn't who I wanted to be and not even close to where I wanted to be—physically, relationally, professionally or spiritually.

Looking back, I can tell you exactly what happened. I had drifted. I was going one direction as an adolescent—when I was fourteen, to be exact—and then my drift began. It wasn't my parents' divorce or getting bullied every day that did it. It was the lie I believed because of those things, the lie that I wasn't worth my parents staying together, that I was nothing but a punching bag for anyone who needed to take a jab at someone. I unknowingly offered myself up to be that "someone," believing the lie that I somehow deserved it.

I was in my early twenties when my first panic attack hit, compounded by years of believing lies about my lack of worth. I was heading to a concert with some friends and sitting in the passenger seat. Adrenaline pumped through every vein in my body and dread raced through every synapse of my brain, causing me to feel completely out of control and out of touch with reality. My arms and legs went numb. Every pore on my face broke into a cold sweat. I wanted to throw up. I gripped the door handle as the conversation in the car turned into a blur of sounds.

I wanted an ejection seat but there was none. I had thought the two decades of life I had lived up to that point were pretty normal, as anyone would define "normal." That car ride was anything but normal, however. Alarms were going off in my head, alerting me that there was a problem—a very, very big problem that necessitated an emergency evacuation from the car. From the situation. From these people. I was either going to pass out, throw up, have a heart attack or all three.

It was nearly a decade later when I went back to examine this incident in an attempt to explore its origin. What I discovered was a paper trail back in time, from the moment when the drift began up to the point of panic that awful night, culminating in my life unraveling into an eight-year panic disorder. It revealed how far off the path I had drifted. In that sense, the drift itself was gradual, although its culmination into a panic attack that night was like a freight train that did not stop for eight long, unforgiving years.

All I knew was that I was not the person I thought I would be, I was not where I thought I should be, and the person I wanted to be was a fairytale. In the words of the famous American actress Mae West, "I used to be Snow White, but I drifted."

I examined the paper trail for clues. There was the fact I never had a girlfriend for more than a month. There were also all the compartmentalized coping mechanisms. Not one single friend or family member was aware of them all. With a certain friend, I disclosed that I drank too much. With another friend, I shared about my panic attacks. My roommate was my sole accountability partner to ask about my bouts with porn. And my friend from Tennessee was the one I talked to about my insecurities. I chose who to disclose what to, but I never told everything to any one person. I just assumed this is what all of us do. This, of course, made me question my own authenticity, as I hid my whole self and my struggles from others.

I continued down the rabbit hole, turning over memories and examining each one for more clues that might lead to the smoking gun of the crime scene—the place where my identity and value was initially assaulted and began to unravel. Where the man I dreamed to be, and what I purposed to do in life, was first fractured, then confused and, ultimately, lost.

I eventually found it one day while writing out the ten worst moments of my life. It was a memory about my parent's divorce I had kept buried. I didn't intentionally bury it because it was painful (although it was); rather, I buried it because I didn't know how to process it. But here I was, face to face with it, deciphering what it meant to me and how it sent me off course. As I dug in and prodded it from different angles, I discovered something significant. At its root, a lie was conceived that I believed about myself.

The lie, which I'll get into in a bit, led me off the path I was on and put me on a destructive autopilot, with multiple medications and coping strategies to fuel my further journey into drift.

Who am I really? I thought to myself. That is the very type of inquiry your drift will pose to your inner soul.

What is my purpose?

Do I contribute?

What was I made for?

Does anything I do really matter?

The drift is meant to lead you astray, away from your true self and from your value, destiny and purpose.

It wasn't my parents' divorce that knocked me off course and sent me into the drift. It was how I processed it, internalized it and began to believe something that wasn't true about myself or my purpose. My agreement with that lie empowered it to become a megaphone in the back of my mind, on repeat, all day, every day, year after year. It followed me everywhere I went and became the lens through which I saw everything—others, life, God and, ultimately, myself.

But it wasn't merely discovering the lie that led to my breakthrough. It's what I did with the lie. I sent it on its miserable way and replaced it with truth that set me on a new trajectory toward breakthrough, freedom, confidence—the path I wanted to be on in the first place. Identifying the lies you have believed will only be helpful when you do the work to start believing and living what's really true.

Change and breakthrough does not miraculously appear out of thin air. What I discovered is that change comes from making a change. But without knowing where we got off course or what caused us to drift, we will continue to treat our symptoms topically, on the surface, and remain in the never-ending cycle of behavior modification.

Thanks, but no thanks.

It is for your breakthrough that I wrote this guide. What I discovered through my story is a blueprint to breakthrough for anyone who has drifted. I believe the stories and examples I share will help you to see the same patterns and trajectory that sent you off course. Part 3 will walk you through exercises to pinpoint what caused you to drift in the first place, and how you can alter the course to get back into the truth of your identity and purpose. The last section asks questions.

I like questions, specifically the ones that everyone wants to ask but are too afraid to ask. Not me; I'm going to ask all of them.

Most of us are not aware of the sea of unconscious thoughts floating in our minds. We are, however, very aware of the feelings and unwanted behaviors that seem to keep us stuck in the past and off course from the future we desire. The questions will help you to identify the events and lies attached to your personal life history that sent you off course in the first place. My hope is that you find the truth and freedom you seek through this guide—your true identity, value and purpose in life. It has worked for me, and for many others as well.

WHAT FEELS TRUE BECOMES TRUE, EVEN IF IT'S NOT

I was like Amanda in a lot of ways, stuck in the gap between **where I was in life** and **who I wanted to be in life**. Amanda didn't become a lawyer because she loved justice. She did it out of necessity to gain her dad's approval. Deep down, she always wanted to become a fashion designer. But that would have only reinforced her dad's disapproval, further reinforcing her feelings of being unwanted.

So, she found a niche in practicing law that allowed her to feel like she was in the fashion scene, but only from afar. She drafted contracts for fashion designers, models and advertising agencies. It gave her a foot in the door to view what her life could have looked like.

I did the same thing. I wanted to be in a band, go on the road, write songs and sing them to the world, because that's what made me come alive. Instead, I settled for booking bands and promoting concerts. This was the "office job" side of that life. It allowed me to vicariously live their life from a safe distance. I was far too scared to face the reality that I would be a total failure if I tried to be the person in the limelight. I could hear my dad's voice in the back of my head: *Son, music is just a hobby.* And so, I believed that voice, and music became just that—a hobby.

It would be easy to blame my dad, but we can't blame our drift on others, as tempting as that may seem. Ironically, blaming my own drift on someone else only exacerbated the drift. I've met many people who had amazing parents, yet they still gave inlets to lies that found a way to sabotage the path they wanted to be on in life. I've also met people whose tragic life circumstances astound me to the point of gratitude that they aren't living under a bridge. Nevertheless, somehow they found a way to rally their identity and passions and are now successful business owners, athletes, parents and leaders.

It's important to realize that if you have drifted, you have unknowingly surrendered control of your future and destiny to wherever the waves of life—the disappointment and opinions of others—have carried you.

The drift takes circumstances and turns them into subjective concepts that determine the lens by which we view reality. If a parent shows you no interest, it feels true that you must not be interesting or worthy of their attention or time. Or perhaps they sent you nonverbal clues, such as putting a rock in your

Christmas stocking, sending the clear and concise message: *This sums up what we think of you.*

My brother watched the disappointment and confusion fall over my face that morning. It had been a tough couple of months for me. We had moved to another state at the beginning of my fourth-grade year. I didn't want to move but my opinion wasn't asked when my dad was relocated for work. Leaving Seymour, Indiana, turned my world upside down. I left an entire school filled with people I considered my best friends and showed up to a new school in Kansas where I was instantly the outlier. I was new and my classmates made it clear they didn't like anyone new. I had a bully from that day until the day I graduated high school. As a ten-year-old, I did not know how to process the grief of moving and missing friends. I didn't know what to do in the face of insecurity, bullying and loneliness. In my inner turmoil, I turned into a turd at home, acting out with angry words and disobedience, annoying my siblings and talking back to my parents.

My brother watched me dig my hand to the bottom of my Christmas stocking to pull up a big, black, shiny rock. Tears filled my eyes in shame as the longing for my parents' attention and approval disappeared into thin air. My brother didn't say a word—not to me, not to our parents. My parents' disapproval was reinforced, my shame increased and I withdrew into myself, feeling more alone than ever.

Life sent me a message that day: Don't you see why everyone picks on you? You're just a bother and should get out of everyone's way.

IT'S NOT YOUR FAULT

When the realization sets in that it wasn't you who took yourself out but the lie that did it, it's usually met with all kinds of emotion. Numbed dreams that were dormant begin to awaken and the heart's desires are unearthed, as you start to feel a sense of possibility of who you can still be. This is like the scene from the movie *Good Will Hunting,* when Will's counselor, Sean Maguire, is thumbing through Will's file and reveals his final conclusion to the seemingly broken life story that sent Will drifting:

> "You see this?" Sean motioned while holding up Will's file of notes he had taken from every session. "It's not your fault."
>
> "Yeah, I know that," Will replies.

Sean takes a step closer to Will and says, "Look at me, son. It's not your fault."

Will agrees with him again and brushes off the meaning to what Sean is trying to convey.

You know what happens next. If you don't, stop reading right now until you have watched the movie.

Will's reality collides with the truth Sean is speaking, as it finally sets in that all his pain, all the verbal, physical and emotional abuse of believing he had been abandoned and rejected was simply...

Not.

His.

Fault.

But he had believed that it was. And that belief determined not only his current reality but also his future path, until he was able to let the lie go and apprehend the truth. In a moment, Will was free from the tyranny that had denied his mathematical genius and held him captive to being nothing more than a janitor. How could he be anything more when he believed the lie that his true identity was being estranged, abandoned, and rejected from his family, and prone to continuing the same cycle of abuse to others for the rest of his life.

It's been over a decade now since I found my way out of the drift, and the remainder of this guide is going to help you out of yours. If it has happened to you, *that's okay.* It has happened to many of us—successful CEOs, baristas, designers, pastors, athletes, mothers and fathers. The drift does not care who you are. It was designed to do one thing: sit you on the sideline of life, tell you to keep quiet and play a small game.

I recently explained the drift to my friend Sara. Her drift is believing that she is not smart enough. I told her confidently that what she was about to discover was going to surprise her. Her immediate response was to roll her eyes: "Yeah, I know the answer is probably, 'But you *are* smart!'"

She wanted to believe that line would save her from sinking even deeper into her insecurities. It is what she's been telling herself for years, and the more she attempted to believe her "I am smart" mantra and failed, the more she drifted. We all come up with these unequivocal truths we think *should* save us, but in the end, they never do—like my fight in the parking lot. Verbal declarations without a true and confident conviction can actually work against you.

I looked at Sara and grinned. Then I said, "The truth goes well beyond that. It will penetrate to the root of the lie and cut off its ugly, self-sabotaging head. The truth is, when you were created, there was special detail at work with you. There were no mistakes. Your design was well thought through and intentional. It is no wonder the foundational core of how you were made is what is at stake right now. Sara, you weren't a mistake."

I looked at her, leaned in and said it again: "Sara, you weren't a mistake." I wasn't saying this to cheer her up or to provide her with a special moment. I was saying it because it was the truth. But to Sara, it hadn't felt true her entire life.

Her eyes filled with tears. It was like the scene from *Good Will Hunting*. Her lie was emerging, rising to the surface and staring back at her. The reason lies feel true is because they make you believe the lie is *just who you are*.

I am a mistake. I am a failure. I am no good. I deserve to be rejected, abandoned, pushed to the side, unwanted, undesirable, bothersome, undervalued and just no good.

On and on, that kind of rubbish talk goes. Fill it in with your own awful narrative.

Maybe you've told yourself, *This is just the hand life dealt me. It's out of my control.* You've never thought beyond your current 9-to-5. Why would you? You probably feel like you *deserve* to be where you're at in life. That's the drift talking. Undetected, undealt with, the drift will take you off course and make you believe all kinds of things about yourself and the world in which you live. It's very subtle for some and more obvious to others.

With time, the effects of your drift will turn into the need to be right or the need to look good. For others, it manifests outwardly as the need to be in control or understood. It might be the need for significance or the impulse to constantly feel like you can fix others. Or it simply becomes *"it,"* whatever *"it"* is.

For some, the drift will drive them to pursue success, ambition, or power, simply to find meaning and feel worthy at any cost. Others will crave affirmation and do anything to avoid criticism. Many of us have not even recognized these conditions in our own lives. You may be more aware of the symptoms these conditions create: anxiety, anger, insecurity, mischief, fill in the blank. The result of drift is complex yet so easily felt and understood.

We cope with these subliminal transcripts that play in our heads through a variety of means. If you've read this far, you may want to insist, "I don't think I have a drift, nor do I have a need to cope because of it." Do this one thing today: ask three of your closest friends what your drift is. Tell them there is nothing out of bounds. Invite them to bring the brutal truth and nothing but the truth. You might get some blank stares, wondering if you're serious, because somehow, it will be so apparent to everyone else in the universe except to you!

A good opening question might be, "What's one thing I should probably change about myself?" Or, "Is there anything you see about me that I may not be aware of?"

Don't be shocked if they tell you that you only talk about yourself. Or that you constantly criticize others. Or maybe they limit how often they want to hang out with you because your insecurities are exhausting to be around. Some may say they've just accepted it's who you are. You are *that* person who pulls their phone out to scroll through social media in the middle of conversations or at dinner. Maybe you've found solace in your world of coping mechanisms because it pulls you out of your unresolved world and into another world.

Your friends are probably afraid to say something because it could be like poking a sleeping bear. The drift is designed to disguise the real you. Are you actually shy or are you believing the lie that you're not smart or good enough? Are you actually afraid of public speaking or are you more afraid that you were created to have a voice and something worth saying? Have you settled for average because it's easier to avoid success and the potential of what failing would mean to you? Do you coast by and dismiss your lofty ideas of a new product, opportunity or company, because you simply do not want to face the real question that haunts you: *Do I have what it takes?*

If you discover an undesirable reality about yourself that has concluded that you don't have what it takes, you will do whatever it takes to avoid situations, relationships and jobs that reinforce that feeling. In many cases, you might even position yourself to fail, just to reinforce the lie you already believe about yourself.

My intention is not to point a finger at where you are in life but to point toward *the person you were meant to be* and *the path you were meant to be on.* My drift stole years of my life. You don't have to let it steal any more of yours.

HOW YOU CAN OVERCOME THE DRIFT

I've created a simple process to help you identify the lies and half-truths that have caused you to drift. I've recognized a common course among people, and it works the same way for everyone:

A thought (whether the truth or a lie) impacts your life and forces you to create a vow, about yourself, others, life and God. These vows impact your life to this day and show up in all kinds of ways. Unprocessed, these vows turn into negative feelings and coping mechanisms. And that is where many of us camp out, trying to change but finding lasting change to be utterly impossible. Very soon, you will see why this is so.

When was the last time you went to a professional therapist or trusted friend and said, "I need help. I'm having all kinds of thoughts." The reality is, we ask for help because we don't like how we feel. Or maybe we have a negative behavior or an addiction that has gotten out of control. All the internal alarms are sounding that tell us something is *off,* and we need relief because what we are doing isn't working!

The goal is to identify what's fueling the feelings and behaviors. It starts by examining what you are thinking. This process will hopefully reveal your pattern of self-sabotage. You will inevitably stay stuck in a cycle of self-sabotage because that is what you *think* you deserve. Self-sabotage only reinforces how you already feel about yourself.

Are you one who has watched your 20s, 30s, and 40s go by, as you have grown more and more comfortable with the pain and disappointment of who you are and where you are in life?

This is not a guide to help you find a mate or a better job. It's to identify the lie that caused you to detach from your valuable identity and drift off course from your purposeful destiny. This guide is to point you toward what you can do to change what you think, how you feel and how you behave.

Not everyone will eventually become a successful entrepreneur, CEO, jazz teacher or hip-hop recording artist. We all start on different roads, and many of us, at some point, have veered off, detoured, and now we are simply in a place of life where we don't want to be.

I've met many "successful" people, successful by standards many of us might use to define success. You might be surprised to learn that many of them would still argue they aren't who they think they should be. Maybe they are exactly where they thought they would be, but there remains an underlying current that feels like a short circuit deep inside.

Wherever you are, whoever you are, let the process I'm about to show you help to bring you clarity and freedom, and help to end the routine of shooting yourself in the foot. This simple process ended an eight-year-long panic disorder for me. Whatever your issue is doesn't matter. These exercises will guide you to identify your drift, examine it face-to-face, and get you back on the course you've always wanted to be on.

The steps are simple but putting it to work is hard. We've labeled ourselves as failures, rejects, unwanted, loners and screw-ups. All this negative self-talk has been playing on repeat in our heads most of our lives. It's not a switch you can just turn off, magically making life become a box of chocolates. It will demand some of your time, but you will not be the same once you see the lies on paper and the way they show up in your life today.

My hope is that this guide will be a *lightbulb* for you as you experience clarity, perspective, hope and vision. How many of us need a clear vision for our lives! Without it, we will let the winds blow us wherever they will. Vision will guide someone like Mae West to restate, "I used to be Snow White, but now I'm more lovely and beautiful than I thought imaginable."

WHAT TO EXPECT

The exercises are simple, powerful and hard work. Let's be honest, we all want to be handed a red pill and a blue pill. We want to believe that we can microwave our moment, and everything will fall into place by simply opening our mouths and swallowing a remedy.

Life doesn't work this way. The reality is this: you stepped through a series of doors that have led you to where and who you are today. We're not going back through those doors because they are in the past. We're going to head in a different direction.

The exercises in this guide are meant to cut ties with the past and discover the truth that is tethered to your future. The past is simply tied to excuses that keep you from any meaningful change.

Once I broke free from my drift, I started asking a question I hadn't thought of in decades: *What do I want to do with my life?* I want to make a difference. I want to have an impact. I'm taking back my life, and I am committed to helping others do the same.

Eliminating my drift liberated me into a world of endless possibilities. I was no longer at the whim of wherever life tossed me. I was a different person, a more motivated person! Do the exercises and put in the work. They will get easier and easier as you do them, and you can apply them to any situation in life moving forward. Okay, let's do this. Are you nervous? Excited? Not sure what to expect? If you are ready to do some work, something will happen.

Join me. I'm living proof that these steps work. We're going to begin by looking for clues...

PART THREE: THE CLUES

"Whatever you think you need will control you."

—Ed Welch

CLUE NUMBER ONE: WHAT DO YOU NEED?

I felt exposed the first time I came across these words from Ed Welch:

> Whatever you think you need controls you.
>
> If we want comfort, we will fear pain.
>
> If we want approval, we will fear criticism.
>
> If we want money, we will fear need.[6]

If you need something from other people—love, acceptance, approval—they hold the key to something very valuable to you. You will live in *fear* that they will not deliver.

Fear essentially says, "I need, but I may not get."

Fear exposes our allegiance.

That thing or person we think we need something from becomes the thing or person we will ultimately fear.

If you have the need to be right, you won't give up until you have defeated your opponent. In a marriage relationship, the need to be right ends in divorce.

If you need respect, people will control you, because they have what you need and, ultimately, you will fear people and their opinions.

If you have the need for affirmation, what people think about you controls you.

If you have the need to look good, people's perception of you controls you.

It all becomes a never-ending game of trying to control the uncontrollable.

Fear, perfectionism and manipulation of others and circumstances will dominate your life.

You will fear people because you cannot control them.

You will feel the need to be perfect because anything less than perfect feels out of control.

In the end, you will do whatever it takes to get what you want.

What are some things you believe you need to be happy?

Think about how those needs show up in your life.

Here's an example:

> To be happy, I need affirmation from people. This shows up when I'm in a social setting. I will name drop or make a comment about something I did in hopes people will affirm me. I also post things about my success on Instagram, constantly checking the comments to see what people say.

Your turn. Don't hold back. What do you need to be happy? Write it out.

ASKING THE WRONG QUESTIONS

Drift often causes us to ask the wrong questions, which leads to wrong answers. Wrong questions demand explanations for why I am not living my best life. They typically start with "why" and end with "me."

Why did they get the promotion and not me?

Why wasn't I invited to that party?

Why do I always get the short end of the stick?

Why did she end up with that guy and not me?

What's wrong with me? Am I not good enough?

"Why why why...me me me?" we demand of ourselves.

All this self-centered navel-gazing keeps us drifting. Life is not happening *to* you, it's happening *for* you. When you see it happening to you, you are a victim. You play the blame game and create excuses for all your "why's" and "me's." It's nothing more than a pity party that gets you nowhere.

Years ago, I was buried in a cloud of uneasy feelings after being let go from a good job I had for over five years. I didn't see it coming. In fact, I thought I was going to get a promotion. I was a hard worker and innovator on the team. I was a self-starter who didn't need handholding. People said the company's culture wouldn't be the same if I wasn't there.

On what I thought was an average Monday morning, I walked in to meet with my boss, only to find he was already waiting for me with our HR guy. My stomach sank about six floors. That is not the kind of meeting you want to walk into. My boss hung his head and couldn't make eye contact with me. "Your position is being eliminated," I was told. That was that. No real explanation. I was handed a severance package and became a by-product of the corporate machine. The meeting was over in four minutes.

Once outside, I sat in my car feeling shock, confusion, loss, sadness, anger—everything you would expect to feel after a massive dose of uncertainty sets in. A swirl of questions went through my head, questions driven by all those feelings. I paused and asked myself my favorite question: *What is the question?*

I immediately answered myself: *Do I have it all together, and do people see me this way?*

That question cornered the lie I was believing and forced it to drop its weapon.

Was the problem that I lost my job? No.

Was the problem that I didn't see it coming? No.

Was the problem that I was just another casualty of the corporate system? No.

The problem was there all along, wrapped in an inconvenient lie. I believed it was easier to play it safe and hide behind a desk job so that I could avoid the personal failure of not going after my dreams because they felt too risky. Risk, at its core, is uncertain, and I hate living in uncertainty.

The drift wants you to stay stuck, afraid, uncertain and unaware of how to discover the remedy.

Here are some questions to give you more clues. As you read each one, ask yourself, *Is this a problem for me?* Don't try to figure out how big or small the problem seems, or how you're going to overcome it. Just check the box if the question resonates with you and move on to the next one. We'll use these clues for a later exercise.

- Do you feel like you're not where you thought you'd be in life?
- Do you feel like you didn't turn out like you wanted?
- Do you have a recurring problem area in your life?
- Do you fear not being good enough?
- Do you fear failure?
- Do you have a fear of success? Are you bored?

- Do you have a need for approval?
- Do you compare yourself to others—with their looks, their success, or how much further ahead they are than you?
- Do you have the need to be right?
- Do you have the need to be in control?
- Do you manipulate circumstances or people so you can be in control?
- Do you have a need to know?
- Do you have the need to look good?
- Do you feel the need to be understood?
- Are you critical of others or of yourself?
- Does it have to be done perfectly or not at all?
- Do you feel uncomfortable in your own skin?
- Do you sometimes think there is something wrong with you?
- Have you had any thoughts of harming yourself or others?
- Do you sometimes wish you were someone else instead of who you are?
- Do you sometimes wish you were dead?
- Do you have other addictions or behaviors that are unwanted?
- If you are honest, are you using substances (drugs or alcohol) to self-medicate?
- Are you overeating to the point that you are gaining weight or possibly becoming obese?
- Are you not eating because you believe you are too fat?
- Do you look in the mirror and want to give yourself the thumbs down?
- Do you compare yourself to others?
- Do you have a need to be competitive?

- Do you often make comments that cut others down?
- Are you often sarcastic and you're not sure why?
- Do you find yourself wondering what people think about you?
- Do you have unwanted feelings—shame, guilt, anxiety, anger, and/or depression?
- Have you ever said you will do anything to not end up like your mother or father, but if you asked your friends, they would say you're just like them?
- Are you anxious?
- Do you have secrets you don't want anyone else to know?
- Do you sometimes wonder if you matter?
- Do you constantly feel like you're not capable of _____? Fill in the blank.
- Do you have a need to know everything?
- Do you wonder if you have what it takes?
- Do you often have the same conversations with people about how you've been done wrong, and you want people to just agree with you?
- Do you feel stuck in the past?

Did you hear any voices in your head second-guessing your answers? *Do I do that? I don't do that. Wait, would someone else say I do that? Surely not. Would they? Ugh!*

The first therapist I ever saw told me, "You're the problem, but you're also the solution!"

I'm the solution, I thought to myself. *If I am the solution, then I'm doomed.*

The therapist handed me some rubber bands and told me to wear one around my wrist. Whenever I felt panic coming on, I was instructed to snap the rubber band to distract myself. If that didn't work, I was then instructed to solve simple math equations in my head—6+11=17, so on and so forth. I did them both at the same time, but with no relief. And no relief quickly spiraled into more panic. As panic set in, I would usually pretend to receive a phone call and then lie, saying that something serious had come up and I needed to leave.

"It didn't work," I told the therapist.

"Well, Justin, let's examine the crime scene every time you have panic attacks. Who is present at all of them?"

Questions like this make me want to ask them a rhetorical question back. Sometimes I did.

"Justin, you're the common denominator at every crime scene. You're the problem, don't you see?"

I'm amazed at how much money some of these guys make delivering the obvious, week after week. Then I would pull out my checkbook, leave it on their desk, and leave, once again defeated.

Let me ask you: *Are you the problem?*

It might feel like you are. *But...are you?*

If you agreed with the statement that you are afraid to fail, then you probably believe *you are a failure*. If you believe you are a failure, then you will also see life through the lens that everything you do or attempt to do will fail, because you believe you're a failure. It's who you are.

Right?

But are you?

It might *feel* true, but *is it true?*

Who decides? Fate? Family? Friends? Life? Boss? God? You?

We end up taking on these self-proclaimed clues as statements of identity that make up the fabric of who we say we are. In the end, if we are not already convinced of our true identity, either the opinions of others or our own accepted lies will define *who we are.*

But what if our conclusions are faulty?

What if they aren't based on fact?

What if we aren't the problem?

What if the problem is the lie we are believing about ourselves or about our situations that got us to where we are?

What if your identity is not how you feel about yourself?

What if **the lie is the problem and the truth is the solution**?

The lie may be inside you, dominating every thought and decision. But you are not the lie. The lie is what formed your beliefs, and your beliefs birthed actions and behaviors (more than likely negative), and negative behaviors usually need an escape route, something to medicate, avoid, and disassociate with in order to cope.

The lie is what caused you to drift.

The truth is what will lead you back.

The question is, are you ready to discover the real truth?

Some of you have run from the truth because you are afraid of what it might say about you.

I ran.

It stole decades of my life too.

If you're ready to go head-to-head with yourself, it's not merely the act of facing your fears and core beliefs about yourself...

It's an invitation to:

Be free.

Gain perspective.

Understand your story.

And to make a change.

Truth will do all of this.

In the next section, we will go through exercises that will guide us to the truth.

PART FOUR:
THE EXERCISES

"Everyone thinks of changing the world, but no one thinks of changing himself."

—Leo Tolstoy

EXERCISE 1: THE WORST MOMENTS

The exercises we are about to do go in succession, so don't skip one. They are going to weave a narrative to help you better understand your story.

For this exercise, write out the ten worst moments of your life. I know, it sounds terrible. Trust me, it will guide you into some revelation of the drift you've been experiencing. Don't be surprised to find that the clues from Part 3 are a result of some of the worst moments of your life. The questions in the previous section should draw a connection to how you feel and think, to events tied to your past. In a later section, we will walk through the process of identifying the lie attached to each one. As a note, if you have more than ten, that's okay.

Write them out. The hurt, the pain, the wound, and the loss.

1.

2.

3.

4.

5.

6.

7.

8.

9.

10.

Let me congratulate you on finishing the first exercise. I think of it like going to the dentist. To me, the worst part of getting a filling is the needle at the beginning. Once that is out of the way, the rest of the procedure is smooth sailing because you can't feel pain! It might not be pleasant, but at least it doesn't hurt!

I won't lie, the first time I wrote out my ten worst moments, I recognized parts of my story that I had not thought about, sat with or processed. Tears filled my eyes as I simply recognized the pain experienced by a little boy who had to figure out life on his own. I felt so much grace and compassion for that little boy. He may have grown up, but that little boy was still a part of me, unresolved in so many ways.

Thank you for being brave enough to dig it up and get it out there. It's never the moment or life event that causes our drift; it's the meaning we attach to it. You're about to discover how beneficial that exercise was for you.

EXERCISE 2: THE LIES

We are going to take our ten worst moments and write out the lie we believed about ourselves because of each one. This exercise might take some time to work through, and you might need help identifying the lies. If you do, ask a trusted friend.

Each lie usually begins as a subtle thought innocently rolling around your head. You may not even be aware of it when it happens. It's the starting point that causes us to either stay on track or begin to drift.

A good guide never takes a fellow traveler where he himself has not gone. I've been there, wrestling with my ten worst moments. And I've stood toe-to-toe with the lies I believed, the very lies that started my drift.

Identifying each of the lies was the first step in freeing myself from the drift. One by one, I systematically identified them in my head. To get free, you'll have to do this, too. And here's how.

MY WORST MOMENT: I had panic attacks from grades 6–8 and became afraid to leave the house. It was one of the scariest things I've gone through. My parents offered me little support, usually saying, "You will grow out of it."

I asked myself this question: *How did it make me feel that my parents—the two people who were supposed to be the safest and most supportive people in my life—did not, could not, or were not willing to help me when I needed it most?*

I felt angry, because they should have know that a twelve-year-old boy had no idea how to manage the stress and pressure of life all alone!

I felt sad, because they did not take the time to help.

I felt the need to have it all together, because I felt I had to earn people's love.

If I must have it all together, then I cannot let anyone see my weaknesses.

If I am weak, then what good am I to others? I'm just in the way.

After writing out a few sentences, a story begins to emerge. I can take that story and simplify it into a sentence or two that feels true for me.

THE LIE: I feel like a nuisance to people, as though I am not worthy of people's time and help when I need it most. In turn, I begin to think that I must earn people's love.

Here's another example:

WORST MOMENT: My parents divorced when I was fourteen. It created a deep sense of worthlessness in me because I must not have been worth them staying together. I just wanted to become invisible so I wouldn't cause any more damage.

THE LIE: Those closest to me will abandon me. If I'm not worth my parents staying together, I must be worthless. If I become invisible, it will solve the problem.

Another example:

WORST MOMENT: My dad said he really wanted a girl and not a boy. They stopped trying after I was born. He didn't even come to my college graduation. I grew up feeling unwanted and rejected.

THE LIE: If I'm perfect and attractive, people will accept me and not reject me.

Do you see how quickly a life moment can turn into a lie that sets you adrift? When we buy into lies about ourselves and the world around us, we begin to operate within false narratives. My parents' divorce became the catalyst for my own efforts to be an invisible man. Had I never identified this, I would have remained stuck in a self-fulfilling panic cycle.

Now it's your turn. This exercise takes bravery and self-analysis. I'm standing on the ledge with you. I've repelled down this mountain face before. But only you can take the first step off the ledge. This is possible. Face the moments, face the lies, and destroy the drift.

Here we go:

WORST MOMENT 1:
_____
_____

The lie:
_____
_____

WORST MOMENT 2:
_____
_____

The lie:
_____
_____

WORST MOMENT 3:
_____
_____

The lie:
_____
_____

WORST MOMENT 4:
_____
_____

The lie:
_____
_____

WORST MOMENT 5:

_____
_____

The lie:

_____
_____

WORST MOMENT 6:

_____
_____

The lie:

_____
_____

WORST MOMENT 7:

_____
_____

The lie:

_____
_____

WORST MOMENT 8:

_____
_____

The lie:

_____
_____

WORST MOMENT 9:

_____
_____

The lie:

_____
_____

WORST MOMENT 10:

_____

_____

The lie:

_____

_____

What a journey you just went on! You braved the unknown, and for that, I am deeply impressed and proud of your hard work. Now that you've been able to identify your worst moments, and the lies connected to them, it's time to name the connection between the lie you believed and the vow you made because of that lie. The vows we make determine how we live our lives and engage with others.

EXERCISE 3: VOWS

A vow is a promise to do something specific. Vows can be a positive and powerful thing—a wedding, for example. People say vows about what they will commit to, how they will act, and how they will face the unknown future.

On the flipside, when something negative or disappointing happens, we make vows to avoid unpleasant things like pain, guilt, shame, rejection, abandonment, the list goes on. These vows are generally from negative experiences, convincing us to make vows that, ultimately, will protect us.

The problem with these vows is they tether our subconscious stream of thought to do the very thing we want to avoid, and in the end, we become the very thing we vowed to avoid!

Have you ever met someone who vows never to become like their parents, and you so desperately want to point out they are virtually clones of them already? Or the person whose heart was broken after a breakup and they spend the next ten years being single because they sabotage every potential relationship that comes along.

I could write a book about this! Oh wait, I am. Why? Because I'm a living, breathing example that you can tear down your unhealthy vows and rebuild them with thoughts and actions that lead to a thriving life.

You probably aren't even aware of the vows you've made but these subconscious commitments are running the show of your life. It's time to uncover them so you can destroy them.

Here's an example:

THE LIE: I am a nuisance to people and not worthy of their time. This makes me feel like I must earn people's love.

The question I would ask myself: *What must I do to avoid this from happening?*

If I am a nuisance, then something must be wrong with me.

If I am not worthy of people's time, then what am I worth?

If people can give me worth, then I am afraid of people because they have what I want. Therefore, people are not safe.

I'm on my own to figure it out.

This pain and insecurity is unbearable. I must do everything in my power to avoid this feeling.

From those thoughts, a vow develops. Let's take a look using the previous example:

VOW: Something is wrong with me and I must keep it a secret. There is no safety in friends or family. I'm on my own to figure out life and nobody can help me. ***I will not let someone hurt me like that ever again.***

Here's another example:

LIE: I am a punching bag for others. People see me as powerless and having nothing to contribute. I'm a nuisance if people just want to pick fights with me for no reason.

VOW: I will become invisible. I will intentionally self-sabotage my life to reinforce the feeling that I am nothing but a nuisance and a punching bag to others. To become invisible, I will become average in every area of my life.

I know it can feel scary to bungee jump into the vows you've made, but it's necessary to break their stronghold on your life. You're doing great; keep going.

We begin with the ten lies formed from your ten worst moments in the previous section, so you can make the connection of how a moment in your life developed into a lie, and how from that lie, a vow was made.

Write out the lies first from Exercise 2, then move on to the vow you made:

LIE 1:
_____
_____

VOW 1:
_____
_____

LIE 2:
_____
_____

VOW 2:
_____
_____

LIE 3:
_____
_____

VOW 3:
_____
_____

LIE 4:
_____
_____

VOW 4:
_____
_____

LIE 5:
_____
_____

VOW 5:
_____
_____

LIE 6:

_____

_____

VOW 6:

_____

_____

LIE 7:

_____

_____

VOW 7:

_____

_____

LIE 8:

_____

_____

VOW 8:

_____

_____

LIE 9:

_____

_____

VOW 9:

_____

_____

LIE 10:

_____

_____

VOW 10:

_____

_____

Are you starting to see the connections? How a single lie can be like a block of cement bricks, fortified by a vow you made to keep the lie intact? I took my vow of being invisible so seriously that, sometimes, I acted like my friends did not see me if I walked by them in public! That might sound absurd, but it's the power of a single lie protected by a vow.

Remember though, we make healthy vows too! We are only addressing the ones that are not helping you, the ones keeping you stuck in your drift. Now that you recognize the vows and promises you've made that are fueling your lies, we're going to learn how they show up in your life.

EXERCISE 4: THE IMPACT

Congratulations again! You are doing some really hard work. You were probably thinking this book would be like a fun, halftime pep talk from the coach, to fire you up and cheer you on. But we are digging in and going beyond the fluff that helps you win games. We are going to win back your life!

Now that you've been able to identify the lies and vows you've made along the way, it's time to learn to recognize how they show up in your life. Our vows form the thoughts we believe about ourselves, others, life, and God. More importantly, they provide the reasons *why* we believe these things.

Do you remember growing up hearing things like, "Sticks and stones can break my bones, but words will never hurt me"? I argue that this little rhyme is just not true. Words *do* hurt.

Words stick to us like super glue. If we mistakenly let words in, because we feel like there may be truth to them, inevitably, they will define us and have a devastating effect that can send us drifting for years or decades.

Here's an example from my personal journey:

LIE: I am a punching bag for others. People see me as powerless and as having nothing to contribute. I must be a nuisance if people just want to pick fights with me for no reason.

VOW: I will become invisible. I will intentionally self-sabotage my life to reinforce the feeling that I am a nuisance and a punching bag to others. To become invisible, I will become average in every area of my life.

There it is. I believed the lie that I deserved to have a bully while growing up. They would hurl insults my way and I would take the abuse. I was a small kid, so I believed there wasn't much I could do about it. I never told my parents because they would only baby me and make me seem even more like a nuisance.

Being bullied shut me down and shut me up. I was completely defenseless. I would ask myself a similar question as in the previous exercises: *How did that make me feel?*

I felt alone. Really alone.

Feeling alone affirmed the lie that maybe there is a reason I'm alone. That thought brought a lot of shame. Guilt says I *did* something wrong. Shame says I *am* something wrong.

From my shame, an imposter emerged. I became the class clown to distract people from seeing my weakness, even if I was the joke.

Here's how it showed up in my life:

IMPACT (HOW IT SHOWS UP IN MY LIFE): I often feel like the brunt of the joke. I do not stand up for myself. I let people step on me because, deep down, I believe there is something wrong with me. I often do the bare minimum, so others do not have high expectations for me. I see myself this way, and my actions reflect that.

Here are a few other examples:

LIE: I am a nuisance to people and not worthy of their time. I feel like I must earn people's love. Something is wrong with me and I must keep it a secret. There is no safety in friends or family.

VOW: I'm on my own to figure out life. Nobody can help me. I will not let anyone hurt me like that ever again.

IMPACT: My M.O. is to isolate and keep my internal struggles to myself. There's not one person who knows everything about me, because if they did, I'm afraid they would not accept me and love me. I feel anxious and insecure in social settings and often keep silent to avoid saying something stupid.

Here's an example from Amanda's life:

LIE: If I'm perfect and beautiful, then people will not reject me.

VOW: I will be perfect and beautiful at any cost.

IMPACT: I'm constantly checking myself in the mirror. My worth feels attached to how many people like me and how successful I am. I'm constantly scrolling through social media to see who liked my posts. It's like a never-ending game I cannot win. I drown in debt from buying the hottest fashions, the latest shoes, the newest beauty craze.

Here we go again, It's your turn. You can do this. No fear, take the leap and face the impact. Remember, the impact is simply how your vows show up in your life:

LIE 1:
_____
_____

VOW 1:
_____
_____

LIE 2:
_____
_____

VOW 2:
_____
_____

LIE 3:
_____
_____

VOW 3:
_____
_____

LIE 4:
___
___

VOW 4:
___
___

LIE 5:
___
___

VOW 5:
___
___

LIE 6:
___
___

VOW 6:
___
___

LIE 7:
___
___

VOW 7:
___
___

LIE 8:
___
___

VOW 8:
___
___

LIE 9:
_____
_____

VOW 9:
_____
_____

LIE 10:
_____
_____

VOW 10:
_____
_____

I remember feeling a deep sense of sadness when I realized how my lies and vows showed up in my life. Until I did these exercises, I was oblivious to the impact they had on my life, every...single...day.

I didn't realize that in the moments I felt frozen, it was because that long ago, a fourteen-year-old boy made a vow that was continuing to show up in my present-day life. I had accepted it as normal that I would be triggered whenever I felt that I had done something wrong and was in trouble, all while being a full-grown man! And so, no, it's not normal!

EXERCISE 5: THE UNWANTED CYCLE

If you have made it this far, you've done some hard, impressive, groundbreaking work! Most people identify feelings really well, but thoughts are where it actually starts. You can't feel without thinking. Your feelings have become so automatic that you almost "skip over" your thoughts—but they are there. And now, it's our job to uncover them and face them.

The truth is, we are so in tune with our feelings and unwanted behaviors that they are usually the primary reason most people seek help from life coaches or therapists. Who goes to counseling because they're out of tune with their thoughts? Nobody! We go to figure out how we can stop feeling what we're feeling. I remember seeing my first counselor and describing how it felt like I was on fire. My anxiety and coping mechanisms were out of control and I wanted them to stop. But it's our thoughts that fuel our feelings and behaviors.

I refer to this as the never-ending, unwanted cycle of negative feelings and behaviors. This cycle, however, is the result of our tightly held lies and vows.

Obviously, not all thoughts are bad. In fact, what we've been doing so far will help you to change your negative thoughts and lies so they don't lead to the negative feelings and unwanted behaviors that negatively impact your life and cause you to drift.

Statements like "You're stupid" or "You're ugly" can penetrate your core *if* you do not know how to separate and process the truth from the lie.

Some of you may argue, "But I *am* stupid! I didn't make it past my sophomore year in high school!" The next two exercises will help you distinguish the difference between what *feels* true and what *is* true. You might *feel* stupid, but stupid *is not* your identity. That's an important distinction that many of us fail to recognize, which is why we drift. What *feels* true forms your set of beliefs, and those beliefs shape how you see the world around you.

Shame is not a good friend to have. If you believe something is fundamentally wrong and broken in you, everything about life will be seen through that lens. For many years, shame stole my real identity and I never got to see the real me. What's worse, my friends and family never got to see the real me either. Instead, it was easier to medicate myself than to deal with it—or so I told myself. Those beliefs became the hotbed of negative behaviors, which, no matter how much I tried, I couldn't seem to escape.

And on the cycle goes.

If you want to break free, you must stop trying to change your negative feelings and unwanted behaviors. If that's all you do, you will remain stuck in the never-ending beachball cycle. In group settings, we use the analogy of what happens when you try to push a beachball under the water. No matter how hard you push, it only pops up as something else. Some stop drinking only to start smoking. Others stop smoking only to turn to sugar. When you focus on changing your behavior, you lose. We must identify our thoughts, which lead to the feelings, and which manifest in behaviors.

Remember Amanda's story? She believed lie: *If I'm perfect and beautiful, then people will accept me.*

The impact it had led Amanda to tell herself, *I'm not desirable if I am not perfect and beautiful. My worth is attached to people seeing me this way.*

She said, "I feel so much anger pent up inside of me that I don't know what to do with it. I struggle with controlling it through not eating, but that leaves me depressed."

She described her cycle of unwanted behavior: "At first, I found that I could control it by not eating. When I was confronted over how unhealthy I looked, I tried managing the internal pain through harming myself. I took medication to curb the anxiety and depression."

Taking medication is not wrong or bad. But in Amanda's case, she was trying to quiet the internal alarm going off that was trying to alert her to the problem: believing she had to be perfect and beautiful to be accepted. There is no medication to fix that.

But truth can.

In this exercise, we're going to identify the unwanted behaviors tied to our lies and feelings. Once you see the connection between the two, we'll focus on the thoughts (or lies) that are fueling the internal alarm that's going off in your head.

Here's an example from my own story:

A THOUGHT (a lie)	VOW	IMPACT (how it shows up in your life)	UNWANTED FEELINGS & BEHAVIORS
I am a nuisance to people and not worthy of their time. This makes me feel as though I must earn people's love.	I'm on my own to figure out life, and nobody can help me. I will not let anyone hurt me like that ever again.	I isolate and keep my internal struggles to myself. I feel anxious and insecure in social settings and often keep silent for fear that I'll say something stupid.	I am a nuisance to people and not worthy of their time. This makes me feel as though I must earn people's love.

And so goes the never-ending cycle.

Remember Amanda? Here's an example from her life:

A THOUGHT (a lie)	VOW	IMPACT (how it shows up in your life)	UNWANTED FEELINGS & BEHAVIORS
If I'm perfect and beautiful, then people will accept me.	I will be perfect and beautiful at any cost.	I'm constantly checking myself in the mirror. My worth feels attached to how many people like me and how successful I am. I'm constantly scrolling through social media to see who liked my posts. I am drowning in debt from buying the newest clothing, the latest shoes, the hottest beauty craze.	I am a nuisance to people and not worthy of their time. This makes me feel as though I must earn people's love.

It's your turn. Fill in the blanks with as many examples as you can. Remember, the purpose is to identify the unwanted feelings and behaviors connected to the thoughts, vows and impact. It might be easier to start this section with your feelings and unwanted behaviors first, then go back to the other exercises and see if you can make some connections.

A THOUGHT (a lie)	VOW

IMPACT (how it shows up in your life)	UNWANTED FEELINGS & BEHAVIORS

EXERCISE 6: WHAT'S THE TRUTH

We are in the homestretch!

Here it is—the big moment. This exercise is the blueprint that led to my personal breakthrough, as well as Amanda's. We're going to take your thoughts (the lies) and discover what is the truth. Often, this is the most difficult step, because we've been believing lies for so long, the truth seems out of reach. This is not going to be an exercise in which we take a lie and simply tell ourselves the opposite of that word: "You're not stupid, you're smart!" That won't produce lasting change in your thought life. And if we are after anything, it's *lasting* change, right?

Expectations matter, and they especially matter for this exercise. Identifying the truth to counter your lies can take time. In fact, all of these steps can take time. The reason they take time is because you have bought another lie: *that what you have believed up to this point is the truth.* Read that again. You have bought the lie that what you have believed up to this point is the truth. And that "imposter truth" has not been working for you. It has led to your drift.

I once heard a poetic story of a young preacher named Martin Luther who taught the same message, week after week, month after month. Finally, he was approached by a confused man who asked, "Martin, why is it you preach the same message week after week? Isn't it time to move on to a new subject?"

Martin's response: "It is because, week after week, I can tell you don't believe what I'm preaching, or else your life would tell me otherwise."

I don't know if the story is true or not, but I resonate with the truth within the story. It was my story. I had identified the truth, but for months, it had little to no effect on my life. I realized my problem was that I didn't believe the truth. It felt easier to believe the lie because that had been the script playing in my head for decades. I began rehearsing the new script of truth every day for nearly six months, and eventually, it paid off with dividends worth more than gold.

I was finally free.

Free from the lies.

Free from the unwanted feelings and coping mechanisms that were causing me to drift so far off the path from who I desperately wanted to be.

The timeline is different for everyone. And it likely takes longer depending on how many lies you believe and how long you've believed them. I wish I could give you a simple equation, such as two lies multiplied by ten years equals twenty months to overcome. It just doesn't work that way.

On the other hand, it may happen quickly for you. Like a blindfold being removed from your eyes, you may suddenly experience a huge "ah-ha" moment. So, it may take significant time and it may not.

We are human beings, complicated with a neural network of chemicals and unique thought passageways.

The reason a lie feels so powerful is because what *feels* true often *becomes true* for us. The reality, however, is that the *real* truth is the trump card. The truth is truer than what *feels* true. What do I mean? Consider this, if you are believing a lie that says you are insignificant, who are you allowing to define your life or give you significance? It's faulty thinking to believe that your circumstances (i.e., job, status, wealth) or others (i.e., your friends, family, boss, coworkers) define your significance. If you have let those things define your significance, then you are in for the bumpiest ride of your life because these circumstances or relationships continually change. Your identity and stability cannot be established on the slippery foundation of circumstances. If they do, you will be faced with challenges every hour of every day for the rest of your life!

In Tony Robbin's documentary *I'm Not Your Guru*, there is a scene at one of his events in which he asks for someone to stand if they have had a thought of suicide. A handful of people stand, and Tony asks one of them, "Why are you suicidal?"

The nervous participant fumbles through words, trying to make sense of a reasonable answer.

Tony asks another question, "Why do you hate yourself?"

The participant begins breathing intensely as he tries to come up with a response. Tony breaks the silence by asking, "Is it the red shoes?"

What?

"Is it the red shoes?" Tony asks, nodding and getting the man to look at the shoes the man is wearing.

Looking down, the man shook his head and said, "No."

Tony breaks the tension by asking again, "Are you sure, because they're [expletive] red."

The man starts laughing, along with the audience. Tony gives him a gentle nudge on his cheek and says, "Don't you be smiling like that. You will [expletive] everything up."

Tony goes on to affirm the man, telling him, "If you would be a little more loving toward yourself, you're going to find you have a lot to give."

That statement struck a chord in the guy, because his face sobered up and he began to hang on Tony's every word. What Tony had uncovered was the lie the man believed: he had nothing to give and, therefore, had nothing to live for.

"You have a lot to give."

There it is: *the truth*. It spoke directly to the lie. At his core, the man believed he had nothing to give. When you believe a lie like that, you create a world in which you survive as a victim, which leads to all kinds of potentially unwanted feelings and behaviors.

We are all like the guy in the red shoes at some point, faced with the uncertain outcome of our thoughts and beliefs. I had to ask myself some hard questions to get to the root of one of my big lies: my perceived worthlessness.

Here is what I discovered:

Earlier, you may remember that I shared about my parents' divorce. Well, my lie was tied directly to that event. Deep down, I thought I could be the hero to save their marriage. When it was apparent the marriage was over, I became lost in a confusing swirl of questions. It led me to the most obvious: *Was I not worth them staying together?*

If I was not worth them saving their marriage, then I am not worth anything. It branded me. It tangled and twisted my thoughts, feelings and behaviors. And it was a complete lie. You can see how, as a young boy, that event branded my life with a lie that I did not know how to process at the time. How does anyone process that on their own at such an early age?

Even after I identified the truth, it was still nothing but words on paper until I put it into action. Sometimes the truth is like handing someone a foreign object. They have no idea what it is or what to do with it. I get it.

Again, what *feels* true often *is* true for you. Feelings are nothing more than that—feelings. They do not accurately reflect the truth.

Let's use my life example again for this exercise:

MY LIE: I'm worthless because my parents divorced.

The lie is obvious, and just staring right at me on the page. If it's a lie that I'm worthless, it begs the question: *How much* ***am*** *I worth?*

The truth is in the answer to that question.

As I dig into my parents' divorce, the lie starts to surface. The truth is that they decided not to stay together. They did not come to me and ask for my input. They did not stack up all the liabilities to determine if they outweighed the benefits of staying together. They decided they did not want to be together. For them, being apart was best.

That truth ended the cosmic debate that had caused me to drift for a decade. The lie had convinced me that I had somehow played a part in my parents not staying together.

But I didn't.

I wasn't responsible for them staying together, and I also wasn't responsible for them separating. They decided, not me. End of story.

There it is. That is the truth. Do you know how liberated I was when I realized I had nothing to do with their divorce? I wanted to shout it from every rooftop, "It's not my fault. *It's not my fault!*"

That truth erased worthlessness from the equation. Still, the question remained: *What **am** I worth?*

I hold the conviction that because I exist, I have incredible worth. By design, I am no accident. That means I have a purpose behind my existence, and I'm either living on purpose or I'm letting the circumstances of life toss me around like a boat drifting at sea. I'm not letting my circumstances define me.

Perhaps the better question to ask is, *Is there a limit to my worth?*

Letting my parents' divorce define my value was a miserable existence.

When I started telling myself, *I am invaluable,* something began to shift. I started drifting back onto the right path. The first thing I noticed was that I started becoming less concerned about what other people thought of me. My worth stopped being defined by others' perceptions of me. Before I knew it, my panic attacks became infrequent, and then, one day, I stopped having them all together.

Do you know how it feels to experience a long winter? Cold, lonely, dark, quiet. And then, one day, you open the front door and, low and behold, it's springtime. Birds are chirping, green leaves are poking out on tree branches. That was my life when the truth started to settle in. Springtime. Refreshment. Revival.

Everything shifted. I became so convinced of my unshakeable worth that I honestly couldn't believe I let a lie rule my life for so long. But no more. Spring was here to stay.

I am invaluable. That's what I am.

Before you set out on your own discovery of truth, here are a few more examples to reflect on:

THE THOUGHT (the lies)	THE TRUTH (whether it feels true or not)
If I'm perfect and beautiful, people will not reject me.	I don't have to be perfect to be accepted. Beauty is how I define it. If it were defined by others, then I would be controlled by how they see me and what they think of me. It's out of my control whether people accept or reject me. It's my choice to care more about what they think about me than what I think of myself or what God thinks of me.
I am a punching bag for others. People see me as powerless and having nothing to contribute.	Bullies are fearful and insecure people who need to pick on someone else to make themselves feel more powerful than they are. People seeing me as powerless is nothing more than a story I've made up.
I am a nuisance to people and not worthy of their time. This makes me feel as if I must earn people's love.	Love is nothing to be earned. It's the reward of taking a risk and being myself. I don't want to have relationships if they are based on doing something rather than being someone.

Now it's your turn:

THE THOUGHT (the lies)	THE TRUTH (whether it feels true or not)

RECESS

"The secret of change is to focus all of your energy not on fighting the old, but on building the new."

—Socrates

YOU'VE DONE IT

You have gone on a journey, and, let me be honest, if you took the courage to write your ten worst moments and you have completed the exercises, you are so far ahead of the game. I meet more people who are stuck in their journeys and have no awareness of how to get unstuck. You are on the path to get the life back you always wanted!

Hopefully, dots have been connected and you have been able to identify some common themes in your story. Some of you may be saying cuss words under your breath because now you are seeing a mound of "stuff" you can no longer avoid.

That's all right.

It's real.

We'll get to it.

Do not worry.

Many people have come to me with a longshot wish: that their negative feelings would just go away at the push of a button. I often start by describing how our bodies have been designed like an alarm system. The alarm, by design, alerts us when something is wrong.

Anxiety is one of them.

Depression is another.

Anger, still another.

Those feelings are an alarm system by design. Our bodies would be doing us a disservice if the alarm was not operating. It alerts us that *"Houston, we have a problem."* Instead of being angry at your alarm, maybe we should enter the code to turn it off. The code is simple: the truth. We must stand toe to toe with our alarms, calmly face them and then, compassionately address them with the truth.

The mind and body are complex.

Super complex.

Our bodies are intricate systems that, by design, alert us when something is wrong. Typically, if a person is to the point that they need to seek professional help, they think the solution is figuring out how to shut off the alarm—the unwanted behaviors and coping mechanisms.

But stop for a second.

What is your alarm system telling you?

Think about it.

My alarm system was going off for eight years! That's 2,920 days. I wanted to take a sharpie and black out every day for 2,920 days on a calendar.

Why?

Because every day was the worst day of my life. My alarm was going off and I did not know how to deactivate it.

I wanted to break it.

I wanted to bite it!

Anything to make it stop.

But nothing worked.

So, I coped.

I escaped.

I took anxiety medication.

I took muscle relaxers.

All in an attempt to make the alarm stop.

I binged alcohol.

I swam in a sea of pornography.

I often did them both at the same time to maximize the numbing.

It only made the internal alarm louder.

But the alarm was trying to alert my attention to something about me and my story.

Our stories contain clues.

I started writing.

I wrote out my feelings. All of them. There were a lot.

Remember the clues section in Part 3? Yeah, that's where I got the list. It was my list.

It was ugly.

I was staring at this list of things I believed about myself. All totaled, I made up a story in my head of faulty little scripts that felt true, so I believed them to be true.

But they weren't.

You're starting to get it, aren't you?

For far too long, I saw life through the lens of every single one of those lies, and it caused me to drift off my path so far that the person I wanted to be was, well...

One big, unimaginable fairytale.

So many years had passed that I couldn't even remember who I wanted to be.

I drew a line down the middle of the page and gave all those ugly statements a bold title on the left side: **LIES.**

Then I drew a title on the right side of the page and gave it a title: **TRUTH.**

It didn't happen overnight, but it happened. It isn't the size of the step that matters, it is the direction. Take one small step in the right direction.

It had taken me a lifetime to get lost in my web of lies and contradictions, and so, I knew it would take some time to get out.

I was seeing it all laid out on paper, the beginning of the end of my drift. These lies. They got me into this mess. I wrote and wrote like a madman. A madman on a hunt for truth. My paper ended up looking like a coach's football playbook. And for the first time in a decade, I was the coach of my own life. Not the lies. Not other people. Not my past.

All this time, I thought life had dealt me a bad hand. But now, I was about to surprise life and maybe even scare myself a little in the process. In a good way.

With all of the lies out of the way, what emerged was a question: *Now what?*

I never saw life as a level playing field or blank canvas.

But it was. It is. For all of us. No matter what cards you think you're holding.

With your lies on the table, you cannot hide behind the excuses any longer. That's what lies are: excuses.

Aren't you tired of living your life from one excuse to the next?

Every drifting person I've met has an excuse for what is holding them back and stopping them from living the life they wanted.

You think I'm making that up?

Ask someone closest to you what excuses you hide behind.

Not enough money. Not enough time. Not enough resources.

Living in the *Land of Not Enough* is a big fat *ZERO*.

It gets you nowhere.

It's time for you to accept the truth: your life means something.

Your life is not an accident and it's not random.

Your future, your purpose, your destiny are all up to the choices you make when you close this book.

You can choose to stay stuck. You can choose the lies.

You can choose to change. You can choose the truth.

You can't change others. But you can change yourself.

Your circumstances don't dictate where you are, who you are or where you need to go.

You're the hero of your story, and your story is not over yet.

Stop thinking about changing the world and start changing yourself.

Leo Tolstoy said that.

Change yourself and the world around you will change.

I said that.

The world doesn't need another counterfeit or clone of someone. It needs you. There is only one version of you, and it is time to change the script and get back to the unique person you started out to be before you drifted into a version of you that is no longer the real you.

Change starts today.

But it was. It is. For all of us. No matter what cards you think you're holding.

With your lies on the table, you cannot hide behind the excuses any longer. That's what lies are: excuses.

Aren't you tired of living your life from one excuse to the next?

Every drifting person I've met has an excuse for what is holding them back and stopping them from living the life they wanted.

You think I'm making that up?

Ask someone closest to you what excuses you hide behind.

Not enough money. Not enough time. Not enough resources.

Living in the *Land of Not Enough* is a big fat *ZERO*.

It gets you nowhere.

It's time for you to accept the truth: your life means something.

Your life is not an accident and it's not random.

Your future, your purpose, your destiny are all up to the choices you make when you close this book.

You can choose to stay stuck. You can choose the lies.

You can choose to change. You can choose the truth.

You can't change others. But you can change yourself.

Your circumstances don't dictate where you are, who you are or where you need to go.

You're the hero of your story, and your story is not over yet.

Stop thinking about changing the world and start changing yourself.

Leo Tolstoy said that.

Change yourself and the world around you will change.

I said that.

The world doesn't need another counterfeit or clone of someone. It needs you. There is only one version of you, and it is time to change the script and get back to the unique person you started out to be before you drifted into a version of you that is no longer the real you.

Change starts today.

PART FIVE: WHAT NEEDS TO CHANGE?

"Knowing my story doesn't change anything. Making a change changes things."

—Me *(a note I made to myself after talking to a friend)*

THE CONTRACT

A number of years ago, I went on a leadership retreat in the mountains with a group of close friends. Over the course of four days, we went through a series of exercises designed to give us clarity and perspective so that we could go to the next level as leaders of our organization, and, more importantly, in life as individuals. All the exercises led up to the final activity we did together—a contract we each wrote about ourselves and declared to everyone else.

There were twelve of us sitting in a big circle. One by one, each person took a turn standing in the middle and reciting their personal contract to the group. We began by stating our name out loud, followed by declarative statements about who we were. It wasn't a description of what we did for work or our major life accomplishments. We were not allowed to list the things that filled our days or any significant relationships in our lives (i.e., "I am a husband to the most amazing wife"). We had to dig deep into how our soul danced for significance and the greater purpose that woke us each day. Our contracts were meant to identify who we were in light of the greater destiny of the impact we were called to have—the stuff that describes *why* we exist and *what* we were created to do.

Sounds easy enough, right?

Well, there was just one catch in how the contract worked. The contract was only sealed when everyone in the room was convinced that you actually believed what you were saying about yourself. When someone was convinced that you believed you were who you said you were, they stood to their feet. The exercise was not over until everyone in the room was standing and aligning with you in your identity and purpose.

Manuél rambled on for more than thirty minutes stating facts about himself, but nothing that inspired any of us to stand, because we weren't convinced he really knew who he was. He fidgeted nervously, looking for the words that would tell us what he thought we wanted to hear. But that's all they were—meaningless words.

The facilitator kept interrupting, "Come on Manuél, *who* are you?!" His voice got louder and louder each time, like a drill sergeant getting impatient that his troops weren't making any headway.

Not a single person had stood yet. There was an awkward uneasiness in the room. Did Manuél know who he was? Did we?

The facilitator walked up to Manuél, put his arms around him, and whispered something in his ear.

Manuél closed his eyes and his head dropped to his chest.

The room was dead silent as we watched him tap into something deep within his being.

He curled his hands into white-knuckled fists, looked up, and opened his eyes. I swear it felt like a lion had emerged. There was something in his eyes that made the hairs on my arm stand up.

I have never experienced anything like what happened next.

Something deep within Manuél emerged and broke the silence.

"My name...

Is...Manuél... Rodriquez.

I am a fierce lover!"

Do you remember the epic scene from the movie *The Princess Bride* when Inigo is about to face Rugen in a sword fight and tells him, "My name is Inigo Montoya. You killed my father. Prepare to die!"

It was like that.

Manuél did not even need to say another word. Every single

one of us stood to our feet, cheering and shouting. We rushed in and lifted him off his feet as if we were going to carry him off the playing field after a great victory. This was the Manuél I had been waiting for as long as I had known him.

I later asked him what the facilitator had whispered to him. He said, "I want to apologize on behalf of the entire world that has never been able to value and see who the real Manuél is. We want to see you now. We need you. Who are you Manuél?"

Those words opened a portal to his soul that day.

We had been void of experiencing the real Manuél because Manuél had only been giving us a superficial version of himself. He had been living out of his drifted self, but everything changed that day he realized, declared, and won his contract.

Acknowledging the cause of your drift does not change anything. Making a change changes things. Knowing who you are is vital when you need to make a change.

The exercises in this guide are meant to give you clarity on your story, and this contract is focused on changing your story by digging deep into the core of who you are.

Begin by being honest with where you currently are in life, then declare who you really are and how you will live from now on.

I would encourage you to read your contract out loud to a group of trusted friends. You can always fool yourself with what you think is true, but you may not be able to fool yourself when an audience watching, especially when they are yelling at you because they are not convinced you believe the words coming out of your mouth.

Here is the contract I wrote about myself: My name is Justin Williams.

I have lived on a merry-go-round of coping mechanisms, which stops today. I will stop going in circles around myself and my issues, and instead, I will advance forward in my identity and purpose. I commit to facing my pain and no longer avoiding it through unhealthy self-medicating habits. I will not hide; I will not play a small game; I will not coast.

The story I've told myself all these years is that I'm not worth standing up for. I have believed that I am a nuisance to people and not worthy of their time. I have also believed that there is something wrong with me, something that must be kept a secret. This drove my desire to be invisible. I am done keeping secrets. I am done being invisible. Everything changes today.

I am owning my story and requiring it to serve and advance me. I am not a victim and I will not blame others. I have made a lot of mistakes but that does not make me a mistake.

Again, my name is Justin Williams.

I have a life worth living, a story worth telling, and help worth giving to others. I am a game-changer. I turn the tables. I am on the offensive to get the most and best out of life, and to help others do the same.

When I walk into a room, the atmosphere shifts. What I have to say matters because I matter.

I will not accept it when the world tells me I'm average, because God does not make average things. I am above average.

When life knocks me down, I get back up and punch back. I look fear in the eye. I will not run and hide. I am confident that I have the winning leg, so "put me in, coach."

I am here for something much bigger than myself. I am a man of vision and character.

I exist to be a transparent storyteller, who inspires people to pioneering action and to soar. I share stories because there is power and breakthrough in mine. I carry a breakthrough that people need. I am not just here for me, but also for you.

Justin

Get a piece of paper and write your contract.

What needs to change? Why do you exist?

Be real. Be raw. Be unafraid.

Write it out.

Convince yourself. Convince others. Convince the world.

Who are you?

FOR FURTHER REFLECTION

This is not a do this/don't do that, try this/don't try that, self-help kind of behavior modification list. The following questions are meant to give you clarity and perspective that can continually keep the truth of your value and purpose in front of you, and to challenge you in practical ways to live daily from your truth. These reflections can serve as a safeguard to keep that drift in check and the imposter at bay.

1. Name someone who can help you stay accountable for changes?

Don't journey alone. A change can be maximized when you voice your desire for change to someone who cares for you and will cheer you on. It might be someone you feel is "safe."

This person needs to know that this is not an easy ask. They need to stick with it and stick with you.

2. Does the way you spend your time need to change? Don't be vague or fluffy here. Get real and honest.

If you're still stuck in the land of excuses, a lot may need to change. If you do not have enough time, then you should consider how the way you spend your time needs to change. Will getting a new job change anything? Could it mean a pay increase that provides you with more resources to make changes? This isn't a self-help guide to help you make more money; it is to help you identify what you *can* change. Nobody is forcing you to spend your time in the manner you currently spend it. Something can change.

3. What's something you could start doing to make a change? Don't think about selling the house or moving to another state! What is a baby step you could take to begin to make a change you want to realize?

Start with moving a small stone today. A year from now, it will look like you moved a mountain. Maybe you need to put your phone in the closet for a week. Maybe it's time to look for a new job or pursue a new career? Maybe you just need to invite a friend over and tell them what you've discovered about your drift. Maybe it's making your bed first thing in the morning to start off your day with success. Maybe it's exercising for the first time in months or years. Brainstorm. Get creative. Change something.

4. **What's a dream you had growing up that you never accomplished? Does it still seem unattainable? What's an excuse (or lie) you have told yourself as to why it has not happened?**

You know how we all grew up hearing "Stop taking yourself so seriously"? What would happen if you actually did the opposite? What would your life look like if you started taking yourself and your desires seriously?

What's your unattainable dream? And what steps can you take today to start moving in that direction. The question is not, "Is it attainable?" The question is, "What is the dream? And what steps can you take to move in that direction?"

5. **Is it true that you are not defined by how you feel? Do you see how your feelings have been a factor in your drift? Identify what you are feeling. Compassionately consider if these feelings are truths or lies.**

Panic felt true for me. Once I was able to see that panic was just the alarm sounding to a deeper problem, I was able to start addressing the problem that caused the feeling. The feeling of panic was valid. It was pointing toward the problem. Don't dog on your feelings. Let them point to truth.

6. **Name one area of your life that has not changed, but you keep thinking will magically change, all on its own?**

What a tough question. Go back and look at it. It could reveal the negative feelings fueling your behaviors. It's the cycle you keep repeating in your head, saying, *I've gotta change this!* But you never do. You know what it is. Write it out!

7. What's one phrase you're going to stop using?

It could be statements like these: I'm going to stop saying, "I'm not where I *should* be in life. I'm not where I *thought* I would be in life. I don't matter. I'm insignificant. You can knock me down. I'm invisible. I don't have what it takes. I am all alone in this."

Go on, write it out:

___

8. Change doesn't just happen like magic. What main areas are you committing to change? Write out what you want to accomplish:

Today:

___

This week:

___

This month:
_____
_____
_____
_____
_____

This year:
_____
_____
_____
_____
_____

In three years:
_____
_____
_____
_____
_____

9. How have you dealt with lies in your past? In what ways could you anticipate your coping mechanisms sabotaging your success when lies present themselves to you in the future?

Have you avoided your pain? Did you avoid the conversation all together? Have you swept it under the rug and decided not to deal with it? Did you let it lead to unwanted behaviors that kept you in the drift? Whatever you tried in the past has not worked. Acknowledge its futility and determine to make a change. Only you know full well how you sabotage your own success, so maybe it's time to acknowledge it and try something different.

10. What part of your current life circumstances is out of your control and cannot change?

We all have things we would like to change but have no control over. However, identifying your truth, knowing your value, and sticking to your contract of change is within your control. This remains constant, whether the circumstances and people around you change or not. Make a list of the things that are out of your control and read your contract again. In the face of what is uncontrollable, reaffirm out loud your commitment to change.

NOW WHAT?

"Now what?" is a good question to ask.

If you are asking that question, it means something *has* changed.

To you, I would suggest to start by sharing your story.

Tell other people.

Friends. Family. Coworkers.

Yeah, coworkers. Those people who only know the 9-to-5 version of you. Let them in on your journey. Who knows? They might open up and tell you about their journey.

What else?

Help people. The exercises in Part 2 should become ingrained in your DNA. Use them to help others identify their drift.

"And then?"

Keep going. Don't stop. This ends a chapter of your life, but a new one is about to begin. Your life is like a never-ending sequel.

Go to whenwedrift.com. It has resources to help you with next steps.

We are always thinking of "what's next" for us too.

What would have been helpful for me once my drift ended would have been a course on "What to do with my life now?"

So, that's where we are heading.

We believe this book, this project, is a never-ending puzzle that we are going to keep piecing together.

The goal is to help as many people as possible identify their drift, stop their drift, and take back the life they wanted.

If you've been with me doing these exercises, then you're well on your way to stopping the drift.

A WORD ABOUT ME

When We Drift came about after I wrote my memoir.

I promise. I did. I wrote a memoir. Two hundred full pages about my life. It all happened by accident. I was writing about something completely different in chapter one, and by chapter two, I inserted my story into the narrative.

I had a good friend read it and give me feedback. He's one of those guys who can see past the fluff and dig into the motivation of why you do what you do.

He said he liked it. That was good.

But then he said the book should start with chapter two—my story.

Then he followed up by asking, "Don't you think you wrote chapter one just to get it out of the way so that you could write about what you really wanted to write about—your story?"

I cringed at the thought of writing a full book about my story. It has too many rabbit holes. It was too intense. I had no major life accomplishments.

But then he put the icing on the cake and concluded, "You know, you don't have to write a book about someone else's success. You can just share your story because it's a really good one."

Wow. The truth. I heard it; I embraced it; I ran with it.

So that's what I did. I started over. Chapter two became chapter one, and that turned into eighteen more chapters filled with my own journey through panic and religion and how I survived.

I sent it off to my editor, who asked me what the book was about…*after* they read it. You never want someone to ask you what your book is about *after* they read it.

I realized that my memoir was the story of my breakthrough, but I hadn't shared the steps I took to get that breakthrough.

So I started another book—this one. I had one simple premise: if the steps and exercises worked to end an eight-year-long drift of panic and anxiety for me, then perhaps they can help others along their journey.

I worked with two dear friends, Christy Bauman (psychotherapist and author) and Hannah Paul, PhD, to make this more than just a book but a project that includes a free assessment to see how far you've drifted. You can take it at whenwedrift.com.

If you have found the steps back to the life you always wanted, let us know.

After all, we are all in this together.

NOTES

1. "Alcoholism by Country 2020," https://worldpopulationreview.com/country-rankings/alcoholism-by-country (accessed June 14, 2020).

2. Alexis Kleinman, "Porn Sites Get More Visitors Each Month Than Netflix, Amazon And Twitter Combined," *The Huffington Post,* May 4, 2013, https://www.huffpost.com/entry/internet-porn-stats_n_3187682 (accessed June 14, 2020).

3. Zach Schonfeld, "Wives Are Cheating 40% More Than They Used to, but Still 70% as Much as Men," *The Atlantic*, July 2, 2013, https://tinyurl.com/yy6ocoqb (accessed June 14, 2020).

4. Hannah Ritchie and Max Roser, "Mental Health," OurWorldinData.org, April 2018, https://tinyurl.com/y4bp2hnm (accessed June 14, 2020)

5. "Facts & Statistics," Anxiety and Depression Association of America, adaa.org, https://tinyurl.com/y5c3gjmr (accessed December 30, 2020).

6. Edward T. Welch, *When People Are Big and God Is Small,* (Phillipsburg, NJ: P&R Publishing, 1997).

www.ingramcontent.com/pod-product-compliance
Lightning Source LLC
Chambersburg PA
CBHW060200050426
42446CB00013B/2922